D1167552

Great Business Letters

in a week

STEVE MORRIS AND
GRAHAM WILLCOCKS

Hodder & Stoughton

A MEMBER OF THE HODDER HEADLINE GROUP

OCLC NO. 498 73579

As the champion of management, the Chartered Management Institute shapes and supports the managers of tomorrow. By sharing intelligent insights and setting standards in management development, the Institute helps to deliver results in a dynamic world.

chartered

management

institute

inspiring leaders

For more information call 01536 204222 or visit www.managers.org.uk

Orders: please contact Bookpoint Ltd, 39 Milton Park, Abingdon, Oxon OX14 4TD.
Telephone: (44) 01235 400414, Fax: (44) 01235 400454. Lines are open from 9.00–6.00, Monday to Saturday, with a 24 hour message answering service. Email address: *orders@bookpoint.co.uk*

British Library Cataloguing in Publication Data
A catalogue record for this title is available from The British Library

ISBN 0 340 84941X

First published	2000
Impression number	10 9 8 7 6 5 4 3 2 1
Year	2007 1006 2005 2004 2003 2002

Copyright © 2000, 2002 Steve Morris and Graham Willcocks

Typeset by SX Composing DTP, Rayleigh, Essex.
Printed in Great Britain for Hodder & Stoughton Educational, a division of Hodder Headline Plc, 338 Euston Road, London NW1 3BH by Cox & Wyman Ltd, Reading, Berkshire.

CONTENTS

Thank you to Chris Baker for editing this edition.

We would also like to thank Phil Rigg and Will Skidelsky for their help.

Most books about business writing give you a set of rules to follow, and a few templates that make any business letter sound pretty much the same.

The idea seems to be that there is a neutral and impersonal tone that conveys the feeling of a business letter accurately. You know the sort of thing – the traditional letter from the bank where the writer says:

> *I refer to your letter of such and such a date. We are prepared to accede to your request for an extended overdraft facility, which can be made available once the required collateral and other security is to hand.*

We don't go along with that. We believe – no, we know from a wide experience in helping businesses create a professional letter-writing style – that this formulaic approach is dead (and if it isn't then we ought to put it out of its misery).

Our view is a simple one – give the customer what they want. And we know they don't want old-fashioned verbiage like the extract above. They expect businesses to write in a way that's professional and proper, but they also want something that is personal, warm and friendly.

> *I have looked at your letter about an overdraft and I am happy to agree. It will be there for you to use as soon as we have sorted out the security.*

This revised version says the same thing and gives everyone the best of both worlds – meeting the customer's preferences while remaining businesslike. There is huge scope for bringing business letters into the twenty-first century without making them too informal or over-familiar. As it happens, more and more organisations and individuals will talk to the world in an open, friendly and constructive way, as equals.

That's what we advocate in this little book.

You'll notice that this book just covers letters and not e-mails. That's because we believe business letters are so crucial that they deserve a book all to themselves.

Think about it . . . and think relationship

To get first-class results we have to look for continuous improvements and examine everyday activities with a fresh and critical eye. Today we explore why this is so important – especially when it comes to writing business letters.

That old familiar feeling

As someone once said, 'familiarity breeds contempt'. In other words, we generally pay least attention to the things we are most used to doing. We repeat the same activities and actions over and over again, without thinking about whether they work, if we could do them better, or even why we're doing them.

It's true across the board. The activities we carry out every day are the ones we don't even think about. Driving a car is a prime example. We get in and slip into automatic pilot from the moment we buckle up our seat-belt. We don't sit there and think, 'It's time to change to fourth gear . . . now I'll touch the brakes and I must stay 34 centimetres away from the line in the centre of the road.' No: it all just happens. We do it so often that it has become second nature. And, at the end of a familiar journey, the chances are you can't even remember half of it.

This is not the way Formula 1 drivers operate. They don't just go out and drive round, oblivious to the world around them. They are always thinking about what they're doing, making small adjustments to improve their performance and their skills.

Modern business letters are Formula 1, because they also take thought and care. A lot of traditional business letters are old bangers, regurgitating the same old stuff that was used yesterday, last week, last year and last century.

Anyone can write excellent business letters, but there is a catch. You have to think about it and develop a fresh perspective on something you almost certainly take for granted. The way you think determines the way you write; and the way that the person you write to feels about your letter and you. Taking your letters for granted is the same as taking for granted the people you're writing to.

Modern and appropriately written business letters actively promote:

- brand personality
- customer loyalty
- a caring image.

Over the week we want to help you write Formula 1 letters, and scrap communication's old bangers.

Why write?

We write letters for two main reasons:

- To get a message over
- To create and foster a relationship.

Getting the message over

Clearly, the first step in getting a message across is for the writer to clarify in their own mind what the message is. That sounds easy, but it doesn't always come across, by any means. It is quite common to find a business letter that doesn't make it clear exactly what it is trying to say, so the reader has to struggle through and work it out. One reason for this is almost certainly in the structure (which we look at on Tuesday) but another major contributor to the problem is convoluted and long-winded language.

Throughout the week there are tips and pointers about style and language, so it makes sense at this early stage to set out some of the main issues in a checklist. We cover everything in the list during the week, and you will see that all the points are straightforward and fairly obvious. But that's the issue about familiarity and contempt: the fact that the key points are self-evident makes it easy to overlook them, and launch in and start to write before thinking.

To get the message over always . . .

- consider breaking some tired old rules (see Monday's chapter)
- use active and positive verbs, instead of passive

ones (Monday)
- make sure your sentences are not too long – one idea for each sentence is the best approach (Tuesday)
- use paragraphs properly, so you don't have long daunting blocks of words facing the reader (Tuesday)
- think about using headings and other editorial techniques (like bullet points) where appropriate (Tuesday)
- give your letter the personal touch with 'you', 'I', and 'we' (Monday).

. . . never . . .

- use jargon a reader may not understand: you recognise the language of your own business, but most people won't (Monday)
- use out of date language you would never use outside a business letter – for instance, *I refer to your communication of yesterday's date*, or *I await the favour of a reply at your earliest convenience* (Monday)

. . . and think hard before

- using Latin words and abbreviations (such as *re., etc., i.e., quid pro quo*), when there's a more friendly English alternative

- using tired old clichés to sign on and sign off (*I am writing to . . ., please do not hesitate to contact me . . .*)
- using two words when one will do, or a long word when there's a perfectly good short one
- using clumsy alternatives rather than repeating a word.

Creating the relationship

Increasingly, there are reasons for writing other than simply to convey information. More and more a business letter is seen as an opportunity to establish or maintain a relationship between the writer and the reader.

Organisations are keen to develop a personality that shines through their letters, so the reader feels comfortable and safe, knowing it's their bank writing to them with a special offer, their supermarket responding to a query, or their airline acknowledging their booking. It's a perfectly normal and respectable way of doing business, based on the very sound notion that repeat business is at least as important as new clients and customers.

These days companies know what you spend from the points you clock up on your loyalty card, and can find out virtually everything about you and your likely buying habits from electronic transactions. And nowadays a good deal of straightforward information is sent instantly down a telephone line, to a voicemail box, a fax or an e-mail address, so there are very few occasions when a simple business letter is quite as simple as it seems.

Don't get us wrong; this is not in itself a bad thing in any way. We know which we'd pick, given a choice between:

- a letter written by someone who clearly tries to make you feel good about them and their company, by making it relevant to you and your needs
- and one where the writer – and presumably the company they work for – clearly couldn't give a toss, or comes across as distant and arrogant.

These are relationship issues that we'll pick up during the week.

It's not just what you say . . . it's the way that you say it
Research shows clearly that people respond more to the way things are said, than what is actually said. The words can be right but if they come across in an impersonal, off-hand or subservient style it's the tone that creates the impression.

For instance, we can say the same thing three ways and these extracts from a letter about late payments do just that. We picked this topic – debt – because it is notoriously difficult to write a letter that maintains a relationship, when one party owes the other money. So the aim is to illustrate that it can be done.

1 *I notice with some concern that you have failed to make yet another due payment. You are aware from our earlier communication that we now have the right to take legal action at this point. We shall do so unless, as a matter of urgency, you make satisfactory representations as to why we should not do so. You have until Friday to contact me.*

2 *I do apologise for troubling you again, but we have no record of your last payment reaching us. We did speak about it before and I wonder if there is a problem we could help you with, even at this late stage, so that we can avoid unnecessary legal issues. If there is anything we can do to help please ring me before Friday, and I am looking forward very much to hearing from you.*

3 *I was sorry to see that you did not make your June payment, and you are now 3 months behind. When we spoke in May I explained what happens if you missed any more payments. We now do have the right to pass the matter to our solicitors, although I would much rather sort it out between ourselves. If you ring me by this Friday we may still be able to avoid legal proceedings.*

The first one is pretty common and is official to the point of being officious. As a factual statement it is correct, but the tone is somewhere between bureaucratic and threatening, arrogant and dismissive, materialistic and completely uncaring.

The second is from someone who hates confrontation. The writer is apologising for asking for what is fair and already agreed – payments on time. This is not the place to be submissive and to creep, so the tone is wrong for this type of letter.

The third asks for money and action, but is one human being talking to another. It is the one most likely to get the recipient to call by Friday, because it explains the position clearly but still treats the reader as an equal, with some dignity. It tries to walk the line between too friendly and too distant in a difficult situation.

It is also the best letter for a very practical reason. Treating someone with respect without being soft is the most likely way to get them to take their responsibilities seriously. A threatening tone may make them agree to pay, but doesn't always mean they will also make the payment. Making a promise they can't keep may relieve the immediate threat. On the other hand a very soft tone doesn't do justice to the seriousness of the problem, so the debtor may think they can get away with it if they keep quiet.

Think 'customer'

This points in the following checklist are not quite as obvious as those in the first one. The points are covered during the week, and they centre on the feelings and emotions that underpin an excellent business letter.

To create and maintain a relationship always . . .

- stand in the reader's shoes and feel how it sounds
- strike a personal note, without getting too chatty and over-familiar
- treat the reader as an equal, a grown-up with a brain
- use a conversational style so the reader can almost hear the words
- think it through and give the reader all the facts and information they need
- aim to help them, or solve their problem
- explain what you are doing/have done, rather than just list your actions
- maintain respect for the reader, keeping things polite and courteous.

. . . and never

- hide behind your processes: *the computer won't* or *your system can't*
- be afraid to say sorry, if you got it wrong
- apologise for things you've wrongly accused of getting wrong
- talk down to the reader and patronise them
- confuse straightforward language with childish language
- treat them as if they are better than you, and crawl to them
- make assumptions about the reader, from too little information
- assume you know what they want

> • leave the reader to make assumptions or fill in the
>   information gaps, when you're explaining what they
>   need to do.

We could say, stick to the points in the checklist and you
won't go far wrong. But we know this is easier said than
done – especially when this is the way you would normally
like to write, but have been told repeatedly by the company
that you do it their way and adopt the style they've always
used for business letters.

We have seen too many situations where teams of people
with excellent writing skills have had their creativity and
spark almost knocked out of them for good by a set of rules
that says you must write like your Victorian forebears – with
no freedom, no personal touch and no informality
whatsoever. The results are often old-fashioned, formal,
stilted and unfriendly letters with a layer of dust over them –
the complete opposite of what customers like and the least
likely to get results and build loyalty.

A traditional business letter produces one half of the desired results, at best. It may get the message across, even if it is in the wrong tone. But it will never help foster positive and constructive relationships.

It's the difference between these two signs.

> *We offer an excellent range of inexpensive clothes for the larger frame.*
>
> *We sell lots of cheap clothes for fat people.*

Links between tone and language

It isn't an either/or situation and just getting the language right is not going to do it. Excellent business letters are more than a couple of hundred carefully chosen words. They must have that extra something that says the writer really means it, but not one of the 'have a nice day' set, where a letter contains phrases that are meant to sound sincere and reassuring but actually have the opposite effect. For instance, *as a valued customer* presumably had some positive effect at some point, but it's been done to death. It is now too common and people see it as a glib line that doesn't really mean anything serious. After all, if I'm not a valued customer, what am I? Who are the customers you don't value?

The customer is the only one who matters
In this case let's take the customer to be the recipient of the business letter. If the aim is to create and develop a relationship, the acid test is whether the letters they receive

have the desired effect. This means that the only measure of success is whether the reader appreciates what they get.

Research shows that the vast majority of customers – people – like welcoming, personal and friendly letters that still have an air of professionalism and decency. Some like very informal letters and a few like the ones they get to be old-style and formal. But the majority in the middle actively prefer a modern style.

So the message here is that any organisation or manager imposing out-dated rules and restrictions on its letters is ignoring customer demand. It may be hard to break out of the old business style that has been passed down the generations inside organisations, but that is what customers want. Never lose sight of that.

What does all of this mean?
The bottom line is not how the writer feels. It is that the message has to be:

> *We genuinely care about you. We're real people who want to get it right for you – because you are a real person too.*

But what you do about it depends who you are and what position you are in.

If you have power or influence inside an organisation and you want to bring that organisation's letters into the 21st century, you have to start with the culture. Just saying that you're abolishing the old rules and allowing everyone to write differently will not produce anything new at all –

except suspicion and uncertainty. The only way forward is to develop a strategy for change, including awareness-raising, examples, training and processes for continuous improvement.

On the other hand, if you want to improve your own letter-writing, you only need to consider our arguments and tips, and then shape your own style. Then you can try the techniques we're putting forward, and review how you're doing.

Summary

Today we have set the scene.

We have looked at the balance needed between the message – via the language – and the tone – which conveys the emotional and personal character of the writer and the organisation.

Tomorrow we move on to explore some of the old rules that most of us were brought up to believe implicitly. And we are no respecters of history because we challenge most of them.

Break some rules

Yesterday we established that not only the content of our letters was important, but also their tone. It's no use getting all the information spot on, if you then bury it in unfriendly language that will alienate your reader.

As a first step we are going to take you back to the classroom.

Picture, if you will, that you are sitting in your English lesson, listening to your teacher laying down the 'never to be broken' rules of grammar – thou shalt not end a sentence with a preposition.

Well, we have some good news. Rather than reminding you of what you musn't do, we are going to tell you what it is okay to do. And it is perfectly acceptable to break some of the rules. (Did you spot the one we just broke? That's right, we started that last sentence with "And" – just imagine your teacher's face!)

We will start with the more straightforward ones and then look at the trickier ones later in the week.

What does a business letter do?

A common mistake, when writing a business letter, is to concentrate only on the style of the letter and forget about what you actually want to say – the purpose of the letter. If you think of a letter as a means to an end, it always helps to keep in mind what you would like the end to be.

One trick that we have found useful is to think about the way you would like someone to talk to you.

It goes without saying that we would all rather deal with someone, be it the manager of our bank or our local supermarket, who is courteous and helpful. Someone who listens to us and treats us like an equal.

We have drawn up a list of how we would want a business associate to speak to us. The left-hand column of the table below shows this list, and the right hand side shows what we wouldn't expect:

Courteous, polite	Abrupt, rude
Listens to customer and understands their needs and concerns	Is only interested in what they have got to say, and doesn't react to the customer
Has a 'human' personality	Speaks and acts like a machine
Talks to us in a way we understand	Uses jargon and tehcnical speak making it hard to understand what they want to tell us

Now there is no reason why this list shouldn't be applied to letters, just as much as face-to-face conversations. A lot of people think that because they are writing a letter, they have to use totally different language. A formal, dusty and beaurocratic language that should have gone out with fares and afro wigs!

You would always set out to make a good impression when you meet someone across a desk, and equally you should always try and do so when you write to them.

This is precisely why style is so crucial. Write in the wrong way – or fail to write in the right way – and the baby goes out with the bathwater; the reader is hung up on the style and doesn't hear your message, so the purpose of the letter is lost.

The difference between a face-to-face encounter and a letter is that it's easier to get the message across, face-to-face. You get instant feedback when you're with someone, and their immediate reactions – facial expressions, body language and spoken comments – help you shape your personal style. You don't have that feedback in a letter, so it's possible to write in the way that you like, without really considering their views, feelings or reactions.

The bad news . . .
We now know what we're aiming for: something warm, open and honest. Something that exudes personality and character, that's bright and cheerful; and maybe even loving and poetic. But let's not get carried away here. It's just business after all.

So what's the problem? Well, writing in an open, friendly tone is not as easy as all that. It is something that needs to be worked on. In fact, it needs a good deal of thought, care and patience. One reason for this is that it is extremely hard to consciously ignore all the rules that have been drummed into us over the years.

Did you spot it? *To consciously ignore:* a split infinitive! At school many of us would have been severely admonished for committing such a crime. But the alternative, *consciously to ignore*, is a bit formal and clumsy to fit with the style we are using to write this book. So we split an infinitive: the world has continued to spin and every reader knows precisely what we meant.

Did you spot that one as well, *But the alternative*? Another 'rule' was never to start a sentence with 'and' or 'but'. Funny, though, that *however, nevertheless* and *notwithstanding that fact* seem to be okay, even though they are essentially another way of saying *but*. Could it be because they are long and impressive sounding word phrases, while poor little *but* is so common?

Teachers, society and bosses have worked really hard to stop anyone writing as individuals, in our own style and with our own slight idiosyncrasies. We have been made to believe that there is one correct way to write, and that anything else is almost a crime.

So it isn't surprising that when we turn up and say you don't have to stick to the rules any more that it takes more than a few minutes to drop the habits of a lifetime.

And the good news . . .
The good news is that it is perfectly possible. Anyone can teach themselves to write better. However, the first thing you've got to realise is the point we were making just now: the way you were taught in the past isn't necessarily the only way – or even the right one.

Rules, rules and more rules

The first thing to say is that some rules *are* important. Without them we couldn't communicate effectively. We have to speak and write in sentences and sentences must have rules. This is a basic fact, and it would be stupid to ignore it.

However, where we have often gone wrong in the past is that we have made grammatical rules seem too important. Or perhaps we have allowed 'experts' to make us feel that they really knew best, while we were pathetically stupid and uneducated because we did not follow their complicated and often totally esoteric diktats. In fact, the rules have become the most important thing about writing.

Spelling and grammar do matter

Before we go any further let us say that we're definitely not arguing that grammar and spelling are unimportant. They are the foundations of sound communication and we're completely in favour. But sometimes they seem to be the only issues that cause a really strong reaction when anyone is examining the use of language, and especially the linguistic standards of school-leavers. Nobody mentions creativity, clarity or the ability to strike a real emotional chord in the reader. No: it's all about pupils who can't spell, and who move on to become employees who can't differentiate between a colon and a semi-colon.

Forget communication; forget expressing what you actually want to say, in the way the customer wants to hear it. The only important thing seems to be that you stick to the correct rules, and get a page full of ticks and stars.

A matter of balance and judgement

Two reasons why rules are useful

- They help us to write clearly
- They help us make sense.

If this happens and we do write clearly and make sense, the reader benefits.

Two reasons why rules are a problem:

- They can encourage stuffiness and pomposity
- They can make us forget to actually communicate.

If this happens we make it hard for the reader to get the message and relate to us as people.

A modest proposal

What we want to suggest is this. While rules have their place, they must ultimately come second to communication and tone. For aren't these things what writing is all about? Rules are important as long as they help us to communicate clearly, in the appropriate language and style.

The questions

But if rules actively prevent us from doing this, we have to ask: what is their value and importance, and why do we give them any thought at all?

The answers

How about if we say that it's only stuffy, conservative people
who would suggest that we must blindly observe all the
rules – the kind of people who like things to stay as they are
just for the sake of it. We could extend the answer and say
that these are the people who write the sort of dusty and
formal business letters that don't fit in today's business
environment. So why should we listen to them?

Then we could go on to say that we throw all the rules away
and do whatever we like. We don't need to think about them.
But we would not dream of going that far, or for one moment
suggest that rules should always be broken or ignored. That
would be just as stupid as obeying rules for the sake of it.

The answer is that the 'rules' of grammar, spelling and
vocabulary do not come as a package. You can stick to those
that make a real positive difference to what you are writing,
and still have some flexibility with those others that cramp
your style.

People in glasshouses

If everyone obeyed all the rules all the time, it might be
harder to suggest breaking a few. But many of the people
who complain loudly about broken rules and slipping
standards are guilty themselves. They break some of the
rules because they are not clear on every tiny aspect of
'correct grammar'.

For instance, how often do you see the word *whilst* used
wrongly? You see something like, *I wrote the letter whilst I was
having a short tea break,* when the correct is *while.* 'While'
means *during the time that,* but 'whilst' does not. It means *even
though,* so the sentence as written says that they wrote the

letter *even though* they were having a break, and not during a few odd minutes when they had nothing else to do.

Or you read, *if it was to be the case,* when the technically correct version uses the subjunctive, *if it were to be the case.*

A leaflet that stuck to the rules

We once wrote a short leaflet to tell people about a particular training course.

At the time we stuck carefully to all the rules, so when it came to 'who' and 'whom' we chose the technically correct option. So the final leaflet had these four headings.

What is the course?   *When does it take place?*
Where is it?   *Why should I attend?*

Then it had this final heading: *For whom is it?*

The result: a technically correct piece of grammar that people said sounded really strange. Quite a few were put off the course because they had the impression that they could look silly, as they didn't talk that way.

When the final heading was reprinted as *Who is it for?* we did not get one complaint about bad grammar, but neither did we get any worried people asking us whether they had the necessary level of grammatical knowledge.

Flexi-write

Writing is like business itself: the key is flexibility. We write letters for many different reasons, to many people in different situations. Every one of those people has a unique personality, and their own unique needs and expectations. It would be a tall order to please every one of them all the time, and if you could do that you'd be very successful indeed. But you can use your judgement to improve things, to start really engaging with the person.

Remember, people appreciate the effort, even when they're disappointed with the overall result – as people who give presents learnt a long time ago. So use judgement and give yourself permission to break a few rules. For example, you may be told that you must never mix singular and plural, so *a manager can develop their team* is wrong, mixing 'a manager' and 'their'. But if you were to write a long document using *his/her* on several occasions, the end result would be a truly cumbersome bit of reading, with the natural flow completely broken.

Old rules of writing, ready for breaking

Rules like these are sometimes quoted as benchmarks of 'proper' business English. You do not have to set out to break them all, but you should feel able to bend them when it adds to the understanding and readability of a letter.

1 Don't use *and* or *but* at the start of a sentence
2 Never split infinitives
3 Never put a comma before 'and'
4 Never use contractions like *don't, isn't, you've* or *won't*
5 Avoid getting personal and do not say *I, we* or *you*
6 Never say sorry: it's a sign of weakness
7 A passive voice is businesslike (*the goods were despatched by*

us . . . the account was rendered to you) but a strong and active one is not

8 The older and more formal the style, the more business-like it sounds

9 Keep it neutral and suppress fun, spark and personality.

If these sound all too familiar, it's time you started looking a bit more closely at this whole question of rules. It's time to start asking what writing is really about. We will explain how you can break the first six at a stroke. The final three are not quite so simple, so we'll look at what they mean today and examine how to break them tomorrow.

That old 'and-but' chestnut
Rule number one in the lexicon of teacher's grammar is:

Don't start a sentence with 'and' or 'but'

You probably remember it well. Perhaps you chanted it parrot fashion in English lessons? Do you also remember those long, awkward constructions you were allowed to use instead *however, on the other hand, in addition*? They said exactly the same thing and sometimes took so long to write out that you'd actually forgotten what you were trying to say by the time you'd finished them.

Well, the good news is, you don't need to use them any more. *And* or *but, so* and *then*, are back and here to stay. Some top experts from one of the most prestigious dictionaries said so recently, so don't let anyone tell you it's wrong.

Split it up
   It's a funny thing, to truly endeavour to keep your infinitives closely together

Poets (even hacks like us) long ago recognised that rules were flexible. It was important that they were, because in poetry the demands of rhyme and rhythm are more important than the odd rule here or there. 'Poetic license' makes sense.

Split infinitives are a classic example of a rule that it is fine to bin, in the interests of general sanity as well as style and rhythm. Poets realised this, and now the rest of the world is waking up to it as well.

What is a split infinitive you may ask? And if that's the case we're certainly not going to tell you. Ignorance is bliss, as they say. But just in case you did have it knocked into you at school, now is the time to quickly punch back – and hard. Split infinitives are alright. Truly, they are.

Then there's the comma, and 'and'
Business writing has to make sense and have clear meaning. Sometimes a sentence just does not work so well if you leave out a comma before *and*. There has always been some

freedom here, using what is technically known as an 'Oxford comma'. We're not going to bore you with a detailed explanation but its purpose is to ensure that a list is straightforward and cannot be misunderstood.

How are the contractions?
Contractions are fine. *It's, can't, won't, we'll* and the other examples of two words being contracted into one with an apostrophe – the ' symbol – all do very nicely in the correct place. It has to depend on the context. Contractions do affect the tone so they need to be used where they sound appropriate. It may be easier to use them in a letter of thanks or praise, than in a letter answering a formal complaint. But you can always switch between contractions and the full versions in the same letter. Again, the important thing is flexibility.

Just to change the tone
We said some rules are up for grabs. Some are very definitely not, and one of the most common mistakes is to use apostrophes wrongly. There is no flexibility here: it is always bad grammar. So *it's* means 'it is', but *its* means 'belonging to' it. And a plural never has an apostrophe: *free meal's, fresh sprout's* do not exist.

It's the personal touch
The rules will tell you to avoid using *I* too often – and certainly to avoid it at the start of a sentence or paragraph. And you may remember being told that it is just not done, to address the reader too directly, with a *you*. The thinking was that it is too self-seeking to push yourself forward like this, and force yourself on someone else. So the personal touch was frowned on, if not actually banned.

But there is no escaping the fact that we are people writing this, and you're a person reading it. You, me, us, them – we all exist. Real messages come from one human being and go to another. They are not abstract and anonymous – they are personal. So we need to think about breaking this rule quite a lot.

Any company which tries to present an anonymous face to its customers is no longer in the know. People actually like human contact and real people, and do not enjoy being kept apart from it by some anonymous machine. And as for letters which almost seem to imply that the reader is more of a number than a person, they're simply disrespectful and rude.

So the message is, relax a bit. Businesses which show a bit of warmth and humanity turn customers on. Those which don't just switch them off. And above all, don't be afraid to step out from behind the corporate veil and prove that there are people in here and that you're one of them.

There's a name at the bottom of the letter you're writing. So why should it be written as if it's from an anonymous or a royal *we*. So say: *I was concerned by your letter* or *I was glad to hear your views*. People are much more likely to believe and trust a single person than they are to trust anonymous collective entities – just as we're more trusting of a real person than a faceless voice.

As a general rule, use:

- *I* if it's something that you have done, or are promising: *I have sent you . . . I can ring again . . . I will make sure that . . .*
- *we* if it is a corporate policy or a wider issue that you do not have personal discretion over: *we do not refund deposits*

unless . . . we have always taken complaints seriously . . . we will consider this when we review the product.

Sorry . . . but we don't apologise
Trying to get an organisation to admit it might be less than perfect has been – and can still be – virtually impossible. It's like politicians talking: never answering the question and giving you a reply that is not related to the question you asked.

Breaking this rule is simple as long as you do not work in a situation where no-one is allowed to admit any human error, even when it's blatantly obvious. And it's almost as bad to have to apologise for something that was not a mistake, but a misunderstanding on the customer's part.

If you are wrong and have done something to offend someone else, just say sorry, upfront and clearly. But we'd suggest you don't apologise when it isn't your fault.

To help with this particularly difficult area of apologies and responses to a complaint, there is more about it tomorrow, and it's an issue we cover in detail on Thursday.

Passive, po-faced and patronising
The last four rules in our list run together. What they have in common is that the old – and still far too current – thinking was that a business letter should convey a sense of gravitas, dignity and weight. It should sound bespectacled, male, bow-tied, pipe-sucking and manual-typing, and should conjure up an image of the office where it was typed – dusty and drowning in seas of paper. Somehow this was all meant to equal professionalism, and maybe it did, once.

To convey this sort of image, letter writers dropped into a style that used certain antique words and phrases, many of which are still used today. You know the sort of thing: *In respect of . . . with regard to the aforementioned . . . hereby, herewith* and *henceforth . . . I remain . . .* All very tweedy and 1920s.

Then, because white-collar work was a cut above manual and other jobs, they had to make sure that they spoke and wrote in a way that made it absolutely clear that this was a senior clerk or a manager. There was status in those jobs, then, and one way of keeping the mystique and the prestige was to use a language no-one else understood properly.

And what better way than to keep the whole thing at arms length, using passive verbs.

> *Your letter has been received, your cheque was despatched and we have been informed that it has been cashed.*

All passive, with no-one doing anything, but events taking place by magic. How much more friendly and post-Victorian to say:

> *I received your letter and sent you the cheque and I notice that you have now cashed it.*

There is no place in today's business world for a stale and distant tone. We no longer have chief clerks sitting at high desks, using ink pens to do double entry book-keeping, or copperplate writing. We have to break away from the flat and emotionless style that our ancestors have bequeathed us, and which we still use. We'll see how to do just that tomorrow.

Summary

Today we have looked at the common rules which block most attempts to write personal and conversational business letters. For most of them – the grammatical ones – there are instant answers, but for the more complex ones we need to take a broader look. That's what we do tomorrow.

Breaking away from the big rules

We have shown you that just by breaking some simple rules, such as *never use contractions* or *never say sorry*, you can immediately give your letters a more personal touch.

From our original list of nine rules, we are now left with three:

> * A passive voice is businesslike: *the goods were despatched by us . . . the account was rendered to you . . .* but a strong and active one is not
> * The older and more formal the style, the more business-like it sounds
> * Keep it neutral and suppress fun, spark and personality.

Today we want to look at each of these, and show you how they contribute to a dusty and tired style of writing.

Take responsibility for your actions

The first of our three rules, which says that a passive voice always sounds more business-like, is probably the most deep-seated illusion among people who write letters.

So it's time to shatter the myth – writing in the passive voice does not a better letter make! Let's firstly remind ourselves of what we mean by the passive and active voice:

I broke the vase (active)

The vase was broken (passive)

Do you see a difference between these two sentences?

While they both give us the same information, the emphasis is shifted. The first sentence actively takes responsibility for breaking the vase. It tells us who has done what to whom (or *what* in this case). In the second sentence, I am not taking any responsibility for what has happened. The vase is broken, but I won't own up to breaking it. You might expect the second version of events from a young child, who is afraid of being told off for breaking something valuable.

If we transfer this to a business context, we see how important this subtle change can be:

Your card has been cancelled, as instructed, and a new one has been sent out to you.

Now this tells the customer what they need to know – that their new card is on the way. However, it says nothing about *who* has cancelled the old card or who will be sending the new one. No one is taking responsibility for doing this.

Now consider the following:

I have cancelled your card, as instructed, and sent you a new one.

This gives exactly the same information, but this time the customer knows who has cancelled their card, and sent them the new one. The person writing the letter has immediately taken responsibility, and if the card doesn't arrive the customer will know who to contact. It takes an important step towards building a relationship with the customer.

Saying this in the passive voice leaves the customer wondering who has done all this. They are told it has been done, but have no idea who has done it. It might just as well have been done by magic! More importantly, it distances the letter writer from what they are writing about – almost as if they aren't willing to admit to cancelling the card.

Perhaps the best way to illustrate this is by looking at the difference between:

We have decided and *The decision has been taken.*

The first takes responsibility, the second looks to deny it at all cost – *The decision was taken, nothing to do with us, and nothing we can do about it.*

You might expect this from a politician when trying to deflect difficult questions away from him/herself but not from your bank manager, telling you why they have closed your account.

So let's look at how to dump the passive, and make it stand out with active and strong verbs, the opposite of passive and weak verbs.

Make it active
Passive verbs are easy to recognise and probably all too familiar. A passive sentence is not too interested in *who* performed the action – so passive verbs make it possible to say something without using a subject pronoun (for example, 'I', 'we', or 'you').

- The money was deposited in the bank.
- The item will be collected on Tuesday afternoon.
- The service was greatly appreciated.

All these sentences have that veil of anonymity which masks responsibility and encourages inertia. *The item will be collected* . . . how and by whom? It makes it sound as if it is going to happen by magic. Make it active and say who will do what.

Our courier will collect . . . reassures the reader that the promised action is going to happen, and that a real person has been asked to do it.

The service was greatly appreciated. Was it, because it doesn't sound it? It's a weak statement with no sense of active appreciation or of real engagement. Why not say it like it is and make it sound real: *I did appreciate what you did for us . . . we all appreciated your help.*

A company that lets its words fall flat is demonstrating a lack of dynamism. Active words convey movement and commitment, and an active individual or team. Image, remember, is all important.

Have a look at this couple of sentences containing passive verbs. What active alternatives could you suggest to bring them up to date? Our suggestions – and a few more examples – are in Saturday's chapter.

- *Your card will be sent to you*
- *I have been informed that it has been arranged that your order will be delivered on Friday*

Strong words

Don't beat around the bush. Use a simple, strong and straightforward verb rather than an unnecessarily long-winded and weak construction. It creates a more energetic feel and it talks directly and without fluff to the reader.

The committee agreed to give its approval means *The committee approved*

The cash will be applied as a credit   means *We will credit your account*

Now try these for yourself, and make them stronger. Our suggestions are in Saturday's chapter, along with a few more examples:

- *We reached the conclusion that . . .*
- *I have given consideration to . . .*

Old style is best

The last two rules to attack are these.

- The older and more formal the style, the more business-like it sounds
- Keep it neutral and suppress fun, spark and personality.

Informal does not mean sloppy

This is the 21 century. It is over 100 years since someone came up with some of the rules and principles that we are looking at. And at that time society was entirely different.

The principles then fitted the way the world was. But today's world has moved on: it's more open, informal and equal. So a business letter should also be more open, informal and equal than it was a century ago.

Informality does not have to mean sloppiness, or a drop in standards. A business letter should conjure up a picture. If nothing else, it should present an image of politeness, respect, sincerity and honesty. Beyond that you might want it to say fast cars, palm trees, jet skis and yachts, or peace and calm.

To break away from the straitjacket of old-fashioned society, make it more spoken. Use a conversational approach, where you write down the words you would say, if you were face to face in conversation. You may need to make some changes but you will find it's a useful starting point.

Avoid that jargon
One issue that puts distance between the writer and the reader is jargon. Some people seem to think that it

demonstrates a cleverness and a degree of professional mystique, to be able to use technical terms and abbreviations that show you're part of an elite group.

Sorry, but it does no such thing.

Jargon is insulting, because it excludes the very person you want to build a relationship with – the customer. And it is confusing, because while you know what it means, they don't. So they will either guess, or switch off and feel stupid – neither of which is a good result.

You may not even realise how much jargon you use, but it does pay to check it critically ourselves. And another way to check is to give your letters to someone in a different line of work. They'll soon tell you because it's easier to spot jargon in someone else's letter than it is to see it in your own. That's because the jargon that you use is specific to your own profession or work and you are used to using it in everyday conversation. Jargon words and phrases are a shorthand between you and other people in the same business.

A few years ago in the staff training business, one could carry on entire conversations using little else but initials: *The TEC, CBI and TUC signed up to MCI and NVQ standards, but IPD and IOD said the RSA IT proposal was OTT.*

Fine, and you may know precisely what it means. But it's complete nonsense to anyone outside the business. Nearer home, and using some real examples from recent letters we have seen, how does an overdraft facility differ from an overdraft? Do you really know the difference between a direct debit and a standing order? Can you explain why the current balance of your bank account is different from the available balance?

These are all words and phrases that banks have used in letters to ordinary people, recently. It's a simple trap to fall into, because the people writing know exactly what they mean, but the poor customer really does not.

So, to bust jargon:

- check your own letters for it – and be critical
- get someone else in another business to check some samples
- never assume that other people share your inside knowledge
- if in doubt, either keep it simple or explain.

Spice it up a little

Letters do not have to be lifeless, dull and free from all excitement.

Aim instead for something simple, direct, and fresh. People respond to enthusiasm and a sense of fun. So even if it's Monday morning and you're feeling terrible, don't let that creep into your prose. The letter's not for your benefit after all. Each business letter you write is a little advert for your company, so why not try and inject a bit of flavour into it, if it seems right?

But always remember who you are writing to. A formal and serious complaint does not generally merit a string of gags, but there have been cases where someone has complained in the form of a poem. You might then decide to reply in a similar vein – recognising that the underlying complaint matters, and so does the substance of your reply.

We're not advocating revolution, just some minor tweaks to add personality.

Instead of:	*It was most pleasing to receive your letter and your compliments about our service*
bring it to life with:	*We were really thrilled to get your letter and to read how pleased you were with what we did.*

Like modern cooking, it isn't only the ingredients and the way they are mixed: it's the presentation as well. So don't be afraid to dress things up occasionally. You can even make people laugh if you want to – as long as it is appropriate. But you must always be careful with humour, and don't overdo it.

Soft and cuddly
We've just been through a remarkable decade in the history of business – the caring sharing '90s. People started to realise something very important, which is that it's okay to bring a touch of sensitivity to business transactions.

Before then it was all tough talk and power suits, and that will always have its place as long as we need dynamism and vision. But nowadays people also expect businesses to have a more human face.

They know that people and organisations make mistakes and they can understand. However, they no longer swallow the pig-headed refusal to accept fault, the blanket abdication of responsibility or the denial of the facts. We are all weary of politicians who never answer the question and manufacturers who never admit to a faulty product.

Never make it up
To gain respect from your audience:

- answer the questions and queries in their letter
- if you don't know, find out or admit you don't know – never guess
- don't be afraid to say sorry.

Dealing properly with queries, mistakes or complaints actually does business a lot of good. Honesty, dignity and some real listening creates a more positive impression than a bland, smooth and evasive response. And there is nothing people dislike more than evasion and excuses.

Summary

Everything we've looked at today points to a style that's a million miles from the staid, formal and passive approach of the old days. We're after conversation, openness, one adult talking to another in the 21[century, trust, listening, and all those soft and intangible characteristics.

A business letter should imitate as far as possible the relaxed, up-front tone of a conversation between two intelligent, honest, and above all equal people. It shouldn't be aggressive, gimmicky, or over-the-top. Don't think tacky salesroom or Dickensian gloom; think spacious, comfortable, modern office where people conduct business in a cool, efficient manner.

If you can get yourself into that frame of mind you'll be half way to writing excellent business letters. You'll be able to pick and choose the rules that we've discussed in this chapter, working out where they apply, and where they don't.

Above all your writing should be about control – controlling those words and making them your tool. Make language your servant – not your master.

Build it well

It is not easy to get the structure right, when writing letters. However you need to build a sound foundation for your letter, before you start writing it.

After all, there is no point using the finest materials and craftmanship, if you start building your house on quicksand!

Unfortunately, many people either don't consider the structure until after they have finished writing, or else forget about it altogether.

You will find that writing a letter and then taking it apart and moving bits around is very time-consuming. Equally, there is little point agonising over the perfect words to use if you still fail to address all the necessary points. If you are totally preoccupied with the words, you will find that you begin to ramble and go off on all sorts of tangents, while skirting around the real issue.

The best way to avoid these pitfalls is to spend some time planning the letter before you start writing. We would recommend that before you write a single word of your letter, you do the following five things:

- list all the points you want to make
- organise them into a sensible order
- work out an opening and a conclusion
- put the middle bit together in clear language
- remember to look at the layout

List the main points

If it's a letter you are initiating, rather than a reply to someone else, there are three steps to take.

1 Identify your objectives. Are you hoping for a particular response? Are you trying to sell them a new service? You are writing for a reason, so remember to keep in mind what that reason is. This will stop you including needless information. It will keep you focussed on exactly what you want to say.

2 Take your overall objective and list the most important points that you want to make. This may involve telling the reader about the benefits of a particular scheme. Or it may be apologising for a mistake and telling the customer what you are going to do about it.

   The reader may get confused or lose interest if you have too many separate points, so try and limit yourself to four.

3 Now take each of these points and note down some key words that will help you convey each point as best you can. Try and avoid clichés, unnecessary adjectives, and gimmicky subtitles. If the body of your text is good enough and clear enough, then you won't need these.

When you are replying to a letter there is one more step that precedes these three.

Always read their letter carefully and list all the points that you will need to address in your reply. By doing this, you will ensure that you don't leave any of their questions unanswered.

Put them in order

The next thing to do is to put your list of points in a logical order.

This might be a chronological sequence – where a series of events are listed, bringing the reader up to date on the current situation.

Alternatively, you might want to prioritise your points in order of importance. A good illustration of this would be a reply to a customer complaint. In this case, the priority is to address the complaint straight away. This may involve an apology or merely an understanding and considered response.

When this is done you can then address the more minor points elsewhere in the letter, or even group them together. We will look at replying to complaint letters in greater detail tomorrow.

A beginning, a middle and an end

As you'd expect, a letter has a beginning, a middle and an ending. The middle bit is where you focus on the information and the detail, but the start and finish are just as important for different reasons.

The opening
Our first impressions are formed within four seconds. So the way a letter starts is crucial, because it sets the tone and can make or break the whole operation.

Above the line
Before starting to string words together take a look at the space at the top of the page, where most business letters have some pretty awful bits and pieces, like

Customer number: 12345
Our ref: ABC/8823098/HG/m
Re: your letter of 13th

The question is, how on earth can we make this more personal and friendly, when we need the information to keep track of the correspondence?

The answer is, make some minor changes that add up to something fairly substantial. This short checklist shows the key points.

- Check you really need all this clutter and guff, and cut whatever you can
- Don't just keep adding references and numbers for your own convenience: the more convenient it is for you, the less friendly it is for the reader
- Don't turn customers into numbers: if it's an account number say so
- Make it human with 'your': *your letter . . . address . . . account number*
- Write it like you'd say it, in words and phrases the reader will recognise
- Avoid words and abbreviations that only exist in business letters, such as:
  – Latin abbreviations: Re: means 'thing'
  – other abbreviations: if it's 'Reference' say so and don't clip it to Ref:

Under the line
The next bit is easy, isn't it?

Dear Sir / Madam / Sir or Madam

Hold it a second, because that's just plain awful. Just think about when you ever call anyone sir or madam outside a business letter and you'll realise it's a hangover from the old days of formal writing. So avoid 'sir' and 'madam' unless it's really the only option left. It may once have been the height of politeness, but these days it sounds archaic and outmoded. In most cases you know the name of the person you're writing to, so use it every time.

An anonymous greeting turns people off straight away, because it shows you can't be bothered to recognise them. Think about the effect it has on you when you receive a letter that starts like this. The only worse crime is to use their name and get it wrong. That really is the end of the relationship.

I am writing . . .

Stop there. The problem is that unless you are very unusual you will recognise this opening as one you see – and maybe use – nearly all the time. So does everyone else reading this book, and everyone who hasn't yet bought a copy. It has become hackneyed and commonplace, and that shows the reader that you (or a computer) are just trotting out a standard phrase. It's not personal and it shows.

And it is a statement of the obvious. Of course you're writing . . . this is a letter, so don't risk insulting their intelligence.

- If you are responding to their letter, say so. *Thank you for your letter* or *I read your letter carefully* or *Pat Straker, our Chief Executive, has asked me to thank you for your letter and look into the points you made.*

- If they wrote with a complaint or you're apologising then make it clear – upfront – that you have recognised their feelings and are taking them seriously: *I was very concerned to read in your letter that . . .*
- If it's a letter you are initiating (not a reply) say why you are writing, but just don't say that you are writing. *I was looking at your account yesterday and noticed . . .* or *I thought you might be interested to know that . . .*

Link this to active and strong verbs
You'll notice in our suggestions that:

- it's all active, and there isn't a single passive verb – there's not one *your letter was received . . .* or *your letter has been passed to me*
- we use names and pronouns – *I will . . . Pat Straker has . . .* to increase the personal touch and keep the commitment strong; it actually sounds as if a real human being has been doing something, is involved and will carry on doing what is needed
- although we have lost the most formal phrases and words, we have not gone too far and abandoned the feeling of respect and politeness; while our suggestions are lighter, more personal, welcoming and open, they do not cross the line and become too familiar.

Closing

It's the same sort of situation at the end of a letter. Recognise these?

Please do not hesitate to contact me . . . and *I look forward to hearing from you*

Of course you do. Whether you see one or both at the foot of a letter they're the equivalent of *I am writing*, but at the end instead of the start.

Sure . . . they were a brave attempt to adopt a friendly and open sign-off, but they have become standard phrases and have lost their sincerity. Like common openings they have turned into *have a nice day* phrases, that get trotted out without any thought.

For *Do not hesitate to contact me* try using the same sentiments, but in a more personalised use.

I hope I have covered everything you asked, but if you do have any other questions I'll be pleased to answer them if you call me on 01888 9987654. Or our helpline team will give you any information you need if you ring them free, on 0800 11111.

For *I look forward to hearing from you* make it more helpful, and explain not just what you're looking forward to, but what they can look forward to as well:

As soon as I get the form back from you I will arrange your loan, so I hope to hear from you in the next few days.

Signing off
A simple point, but sign off with your forename as well as your surname – and print it out underneath your signature. And if there's a risk that the reader will be confused or concerned about how to address you – especially if you are a woman and could be Mrs., Ms. or Miss – think about adding that in brackets. You may not worry what they call you, but some people writing back to you would be concerned not to get it wrong, and could get anxious.

The meat is in the middle

You have worked out the introduction, planned the sort of
sign-off you want, and have sorted out the main points you
want to make into a sensible order. It is now fairly
straightforward to fill in the centre, as long as you remember
a few important points:

- Use normal words and phrases that make things
  clear
- Try and talk to the reader, rather than write at them
- Avoid jargon and technicalities they may not
  understand
- Check the layout and make sure it helps rather than
  hinders the message.

Let's take these one at a time.

Normal words for normal people
We don't know why it happens, but when someone starts
writing a business letter they generally stop using normal

language and start looking for long and formal words, complex phrases and passive verbs.

Your letter was received by us yesterday and I am writing to inform you that the request you submitted for a claim under our extended warranty has been passed to our customer service section. Your request will be given due consideration and a response will be sent to you within the time limits stated in paragraph 14a of your warranty documentation.

Now, who ever speaks like that? And why does someone abandon their everyday skill in communicating clearly with another human being, to produce something distant, dusty and completely impersonal. It's as if the letter *has* to sound legal.

But it doesn't. Someone has written in with a simple query and wants an answer . . . and the answer is:

Thank you for your letter about claiming under your extended warranty. I have passed it on to our customer services team and they are looking into it for you now. They will let you know the result within seven days.

Think simple

Instead of looking for long-winded and clever-sounding words and phrases, use the ones that everyone understands and is comfortable with. We're not saying that you must use some words and not others, because it depends on the context. For instance, if you're writing to an accountant you can use technical accounting terminology – but not if your reader is not an accountant, and not in the know.

The point is that you should always look at the words and phrases you pick, check that they are the most straightforward you can find, and make sure that they do the job in this particular context for this particular reader.

So what could you say – or would you normally say anywhere but in a business letter – instead of these words and phrases?

• therefore	• endeavour	• for the duration of
• concerning	• signify	• purchase [verb]
• henceforth	• subsequent to	• utilise

It all depends
There are no right or wrong answers, and it all depends on the situation. But how about these, as starters for 10. (There are more on Saturday).

• therefore	*so*
• concerning	*about*
• henceforth	*in future*
• endeavour	*try*
• signify	*mean*
• subsequent to	*after*
• for the duration of	*throughout*
• purchase [verb]	*buy*
• utilise	*use*

Now, this is not rocket science; in fact it's almost the opposite . . . simplifying rather than making more technical.

The words in italics are perfectly good words, in use every day and understood by virtually all the population. But the originals are not used so much, if at all, in everyday communication, except in business letters. And there is much more scope for a reader to get the wrong impression, misunderstand the meaning or feel that the writer is much more clever than they are. None of these is a good result.

Now make it look good

Having worked to get the right words and phrases together to cover all the important points, don't go and spoil it now by cramming it all together. Here are some pointers to making a letter easy to read, follow and understand:

- Allow some white space around the lines and paragraphs
- Have one idea in each sentence, and keep sentences short
- Break up the letter into paragraphs, with each paragraph looking at only one theme (related sentences of one idea each)
- Use headings and bullet points if possible and appropriate; the aim is to convey information so it makes sense, and if techniques like these help then use them.

Have a look at the difference these pointers can make. The words in the two boxes are exactly the same. The only difference is the layout, and although it may look like a small change, when you multiply it across a longer letter it makes a considerable difference to the ease with which the reader can follow the points you are making, and understand your message.

Before

Thank you for your letter about our charges and your question about why we charged you £6 instead of the normal £3. This was because your cheque was post-dated, and we charge the £3 excess for any cheque that is post-dated by more than four days past the date we receive it, drawn on a bank that is based in another country, or made out incorrectly.

After

Thank you for your letter about our charges and your question about why we charged you £6 instead of the normal £3.

This was because your cheque was post-dated, and we charge the £3 excess for any cheque that is:

- post-dated by more than four days past the date we receive it
- drawn on a different bank that is based in another country, or
- made out incorrectly.

Summary

Today we have looked at structuring a letter, from the bits at the top before the real letter starts, through the introduction and right down to the sign-off.

We have explored the importance of the way you start and end a letter, and have looked at some of the main features of layout that make a difference.

Handling complaints

It happens in every business and it's as inevitable as the sun rising. That's right – that horrible, stinking customer complaint letter, hot off the press with the steam still rising from it.

So that we can tackle these constructively without getting upset, let's start today by listing five important points about complaints that often get overlooked. Then we will look at each one in turn.

1 Complaints are free market research. They tell you things that upset customers – whether or not they are real or imagined problems – so they tell you areas where you can raise customer satisfaction at a stroke.
2 Some complaints are justified, so the complainant deserves recompense – at least a sincere apology
3 Unjustified complaints – that arise from a misunderstanding on the customer's part – are real to the customer. In 99% of cases they wouldn't have written unless they truly believed they were right, so you have to take it seriously
4 Most people don't want blood; they're perfectly satisfied if you:
   – listen to them carefully
   – give them a decent explanation and offer an apology, if appropriate
   – recognise that they may have told you something you didn't know
5 Getting defensive doesn't work. Even if you are

telling the truth the customer sees it as mealy-
mouthed excuses.

Free information

We really do know someone who went to a shop and asked
for some small cigars, to be told, 'Sorry. I keep telling people
– there's no demand'.

This is a simple proposition: if people keep telling you the
same thing, look at it carefully. There is probably something
wrong and spending a few minutes sorting it out means you
won't have disappointed customers and you won't have to
keep trotting out the same lame excuse.

Take it on the chin

Complaints fall into two broad types: justified and
unjustified. The customer is not always right, but they have a

right to proper treatment. There are a few – very few – 'professional complainers', who set out to find the smallest fault and then enjoy writing to organisations demanding action. And we can't do much about them, except to acknowledge that they exist and accept that the vast majority of people only put pen to paper when they genuinely believe they have a grievance. They may be mistaken but their perception is that they have been hard done by; and their perception is what matters.

So it simply doesn't matter whether it's a genuine complaint or an imagined one. Everyone is entitled to the same basic respect. If a letter is vitriolic and pretty abusive it is more likely that the customer feels dreadfully angry and upset than that they are normally foul-mouthed. A really mature business handles all complaints in the same efficient, calm and sensitive way.

A make or break situation
By the time a customer reaches the stage of writing to a company, you can be sure that he or she will think that they have a very good reason for doing so. In general, people don't write letters about minor niggles or concerns, although there's no set of rules to determine what is important. One person's crisis is another's storm in a teacup, and you have to accept that this is important enough to them to make them spend time writing, and spend money on a stamp.

You know, then, that if you do receive a letter, it is a pretty important matter for the person who has sent it, and that it is even more important for you. In fact, it may be a matter of keeping or losing that customer's business. And that, no matter how big the company, is too important to be ignored.

Customers are what make a business. You need them all!

On target, not off the peg
Customer complaints, therefore, are an essential strategic business area where the results have to be on target, every time. Unfortunately, not enough businesses think that this should be the case, and the department responsible for responding to complaints feels like a poor relation – disposable and basically irrelevant to the real work of the company. It's not difficult to see why, because it can be hard to quantify the value of an effective complaint-handling team.

Executives understandably concentrate on getting performance right in the first place, so there are fewer complaints to respond to. Their view is that devoting time and money to responding to complaints is a self-fulfilling prophecy. The more you spend, the more you take away from other areas of the business, so the more complaints you're going to get!

Their logic is faultless, and if this process of continuous improvement really happens then it does cut complaints. But it is not either/or. It is essential to take a professional line on quality improvement and an equally professional line on complaints. They are both serious business issues. Failing to take complaint-handling seriously makes it seem like little more than an exercise in damage limitation, and a pretty ineffectual one at that.

Complaints are serious

We suggest that business needs to develop an entirely new

understanding of the role of handling complaints. It's time to inject a little positive thinking into what is in danger otherwise of becoming a dangerously neglected area.

Here are a few more key truths about complaint letters:

- Complaints are inevitable, no matter how good the business. You can't please everyone, and some people are impossible to please.
- Complaints are an opportunity to surprise the customer – show them that your business has that bit extra over its rivals.
- A well handled complaint helps consolidate a relationship. People feel good about being listened to and they tell their friends.
- A botched response enlarges the already unfavourable impression. It sends a wavering customer out of the door for good. And they tell their friends
- The difference between a knock-out and a cock-up is not down to time and money. It is down to care, understanding and the right use of language.

There's nothing new under the sun
That's right. It's those same basic principles again. The building blocks of the successful business relationship are the language and the tone; and they add the extra bit of class that makes a priceless difference.

The ability to deploy language effectively is the all-important – and all-too-often neglected – weapon in the arsenal of your business's equipment. On-target words do more than anything else to win the hearts and loyalty of customers. And as far as complaints go, they make it possible to retrieve the unretrievable.

Do something . . . now
The first and most important rule of thumb for handling complaints is to reply as quickly as possible. Do not ignore it and hope it will go away, or leave it for another day. And it doesn't matter what kind of letter you're replying to. We all know the temptation of putting those horrible, 'tricky' letters in a different pile, marked 'To be dealt with eventually'. As soon as you do that, you're slipping into the fatal mentality of negativity and inertia. So be positive! Answer the difficult ones first thing in the morning, when your mind is at its most engaged.

But we can hear the cries from here. 'There are too many . . . I've got too much to do . . . it takes time to find out what really happened . . . I need time to put a decent response together'. Okay, if it's physically impossible to send a full reply immediately, send a short, standard holding letter return of post, that says:

Thank you very much for writing to us. It is important that

we can give your query the attention it deserves, so I'd like to spend a bit of time looking into it.

Then I will be in touch with a full reply as soon as I can, definitely within a fortnight. Thank you for your patience.

And that's all you need do – apart from the essential need to follow up on your promise and make sure they do get a full reply in time. But for now you've cleared the air a bit and bought yourself a bit of time. You have not yet solved the problem, but the customer will be impressed by the speed of the reply and the fact that you are obviously paying attention to it. That little seed of customer satisfaction will already be sown and your job will be that much easier for it.

Getting down to the real issues

The time has come to write a reply. You have done the investigation and worked out the key points in your answer, to match all the issues they raised. So how do we go about responding?

Let's start with a checklist. What are the things that really count when it comes to responding to someone who is upset and/or angry, whether or not they really do have a case?

- Empathise: remember whose point of view matters most
- Say sorry, if needed: it's more grown up than blanket denial
- Express regret, if they are wrong but feel bad
- Be – and sound – genuine: it's that all-important middle way between offhand and patronising
- Tell the truth: it is respectful and it saves you getting found out later
- Say no: if it's got to be done, don't be a shrinking violet
- Crack the code: sometimes there's more to the complaint than meets the eye so be a good detective
- Sound human: if your response is mechanical it won't make an impact. Don't be scared of a little bit of personality.

No one understands me!
Empathy is when you put yourself in their shoes and feel where they pinch. It means not defending the company line, but imagining how you would feel if you had experienced what they did. You may find it hard to do, but you must practice empathy and try to apply it. It's an old truth that people who make the effort to understand others win more friends than those that don't, and the ability to empathise is a direct ticket to the hearts of others – especially with complaints.

There is an open goal here, because the most common experience people have when they send a complaint is either to get no reply at all, or to receive an off-hand or aggressive letter that denies it could ever have happened. So they have very low expectations, and when you send a respectful letter that shows you listened and saw things from their point of view, you're already in credit. Remember:

- a customer who has resorted to complaining will probably already be in a touchy, over-sensitive frame of mind
- they believe they have a genuine point to make, and will not accept a simple denial (why should they?)
- any misunderstanding or insensitivity to their concerns will make matters a whole lot worse, and add personal offence to more generalised dissatisfaction.

The nitty-gritty of responding to a complaint

This is not a set of rules, or an infallible guide, because every complaint is different. But it will get you geared to those crucial issues you're dealing with and it will get you in the mind-frame to really bust those complaints!

1   Take time to think and find out
Before launching into the main body of the response, read their letter very carefully and do a spot of thinking about the actual substance of the complaint. Remember, the customer is unhappy about a specific thing: a product being faulty or unavailable, the lack of professionalism of company staff, a feeling that they've been ripped off. So make the effort to really work out what the problem is and what would constitute an acceptable answer to their queries.

If you need to check details with colleagues, don't hesitate to do so. Don't guess, or make assumptions – they'll only catch up with you later. Once you've done the thinking and analysed the complaint, you're ready to get cracking on the reply.

2 *Express your concern*

Don't run for cover. Stand tall, and take whatever's coming to you on the chin. Say sorry – or express regret – for the fact that the customer has felt the need to complain. You may recall that one of the rules we challenged on Monday was that you never say sorry. Well, that does not mean that you apologise when you have done nothing wrong. What matters is that you empathise.

You can say you understand without apologising, so if the complaint is about a misunderstanding you can still say you feel sorry, without apologising. The difference is in what you are saying sorry about. These first two are straight admissions of guilt, and if they're appropriate, then fine: use them.

> *I am sorry we didn't keep our promise* or
> *I do apologise that we opened late*

If the complaint is a misunderstanding you still need to show you are concerned for their feelings without admitting something that did not happen. The suggestions below demonstrate empathy, but are both neutral enough to avoid either giving in unnecessarily, or becoming antagonistic.

> *I am sorry that you feel upset about this* or
> *I was most concerned to read that you were unhappy about*

3 *Be specific*

Say exactly what it is that you are sorry about. This is crucial.
It's the ability to be direct, to answer the complaint on its
own terms. So don't try to smother your apology in mealy-
mouthed phrases. If someone has written to say that their
loan payments have been taken from their bank account
twice, because your instructions are unclear, don't say:

> *Perrywick & Co would like to express their regret at the fact
> that in recent dealings with them you have had cause for
> concern.*

Instead be up-front, clear and direct, and answer their points.

> *I was very concerned to read that you found the terms of the
> loan repayments confusing. I can assure you it wasn't our
> intention to mislead you in any way.*

4 *Explain*

Saying you are sorry without any explanation and/or
recompense is far too weak to be any use, as this example
shows.

> *Dear . . .*
> *I am very sorry we overcharged you. We don't normally do
> this and I apologise it happened to you.*
> *Yours sincerely . . .*

In the imaginary world of the ideal customer complaint
department, you will be able to answer every single letter
with a perfectly reasonable, water-tight explanation of the
issue or question in hand.

Here's an example in the style of an upmarket food-store
answering a query/complaint about a sudden rise in the

price of Antarctic sea bass. The answer builds on all the points we've looked at so far this week – structure, honestly, clarity and openness, in particular.

Thank you for your letter about the price of sea bass.	Opens with a 'thank you'
I am sorry that you felt we were overcharging for this item, but I can assure you that our policy is to keep prices reasonable and fair.	Clear, honest statement and an expression of regret rather than an apology
At the same time, we aim to offer our customers high-quality items that aren't available elsewhere. As we are a small store this means we often have to buy perishable goods in small quantities.	Open and frank explanation about our policy, supported by a statement about what is special about us
Unfortunately these products tend to be particularly vulnerable to market fluctuations. So sometimes we have to pay – and charge – more on a short-term basis, in order to offer a particular item at all. This is what happened with Antarctic sea-bass.	No apology – this is what happened; it costs us more to buy it, so if it is to be in stock we pay more and have to pass the price increase on.
Since then the price has returned to normal and it is now back to the same level as this time last year.	The good news: we drop prices as well as raise them
I hope this explains exactly what happened, but if you have any other questions I will be happy to answer them for you.	Thanks for writing: we do care and I'm glad you wrote

So how was that? It was one adult talking to another, assuming they have a brain and giving open and honest answers, without apologising for something beyond their control. Only the most unreasonable customer could argue that they haven't been dealt with fairly.

Caught with your hand in the cookie jar

The trouble is that sometimes there is no such neat and logical explanation. Maybe a normally polite staff member suddenly shows a flash of impatience or treats someone badly. Perhaps an item is not in stock, when you've advertised it as a special offer. In cases like these it is a genuine failing on the company's part.

If it is, own up. Do not even attempt to talk yourself out of it and, as they say, when you're down a hole, stop digging. The difference between an explanation and an excuse is whether it is the truth.

Explaining is fine, but making excuses simply does not pay. So, if the fact is that something was wrong:

- say so and apologise
- assure the customer that you are genuinely concerned about it
- thank them for bringing it to your attention
- explain what you'll do to make sure it doesn't happen again
- make a gesture of recompense if it's appropriate.

Here's an example.

> *Thank you for your letter. I was very concerned to hear that you were told you could not use a voucher for that product. It was our mistake and I apologise on behalf of Grace Brothers. The problem arose because we had not issued the right instructions to our till staff.*

> *Thank you for taking the trouble to tell us about it, because it has allowed us to put it right for the future. I have passed the details to our pricing managers and they will look carefully at the way we inform stores about these offers.*

> *Please accept this voucher as a small token of our thanks, and*

to make up for the inconvenience and embarrassment.

This letter:

- opens strongly, with an empathetic statement that says we listen and care
- goes on to say sorry, we got it wrong (which the customer knows)
- shows trust and respect – sharing inside knowledge with them about our business proves we take their comments seriously, and see them as constructive, and that will make the customer feel good (quite rightly)
- offers physical proof that we take this seriously – any tangible recompense (even a £2 voucher) demonstrates a real respect for their point of view
- builds the relationship, through a strong ending that owns up, and talks like one adult in conversation with another adult.

This is what we mean when we say complaint letters are free market research. By listening we have learnt something valuable, which we can use to prevent customers feeling unhappy in future. And not only is it painless to write a reply like this – it gives you one very happy customer.

Summary

Today we have looked at letters of complaint, and tried to show how they can be a powerful tool for building a relationship, rather than a negative experience.

Turning a complaint into a victory is not that hard if you take care in the way you handle it.

The secret lies in the way you treat the complainant; show empathy, respect and a willingness to listen and you're halfway to solving the problem. Use the right language and tone when you reply and you reach the finish line as a winner.

Direct mail doesn't have to be junk mail

Direct or aggressive

Direct mail is a letter that comes to you direct from someone else. It normally tries to interest you in their products and services and it is likely to be an aggressive hard sell, rather than merely direct.

Recognise this?

> *Dear Head of the Family*
>
> *Have you ever stopped to think how you'd feel if your loved one didn't come home tonight, because they were crushed by a bus and killed?*
>
> *A horrendous thought – but it could happen. And if it did, you'd be left not just with the grief, but also the anxiety of unpayable bills. It could mean the threat of financial ruin, for you and your innocent young children.*
>
> *It's because we care that we've designed our WundaLife Accidental Death Plan* . . . just for you. Sign up by Tuesday, and we'll throw in Purchase Protection COMPLETELY FREE of charge**. And don't forget, you also benefit from . . .*

We've all suffered from the curse of bad direct mail. On most days your doormat is covered in it. Those letters that shout at you as though you're STUPID. They're breathless in their excitement as they offer you a fabulous plastic pen, travel alarm clock or some other patronising bauble, to make a hugely serious decision and take up their expensive service.

JOIN UP NOW & THE
REST IS YOURS!

Worse, they adopt a false and offensive familiarity as though you're a personal mate. And they write in long, ungrammatical sentences and use TOO MANY CAPITAL LETTERS and !!!!??s to *make their point,* sending your eyeballs into spasm and reminding you once again with a *P.S. (Don't forget!!!)* and ending on a ****Not applicable to people aged 16-70,* to exclude you from the benefits they've just thrust in your face.

Here's another common style, dispensing with the dramatic scene-setting opening and going for a more directly hucksterish approach:

Dear Valued Customer

*Yes . . . you **are** a valued customer, and that means you are a discerning shopper, too. I know that you already appreciate the great quality of our products. And I'm equally sure you'll want to take up our offer of a new subscription to Hi! magazine, for a friend.*

There's no pressure; thanks to our easy payment options, you

*can send your cheque TODAY or leave it until tomorrow! But
no later, or you may be too late. We've enclosed a **FREE** pen
for you to fill out the form, too!! To make sure you don't miss
out, do it **NOW**!! . . .*

The presumption in these letters is astounding – the writer
miraculously knows what you think of the product.
Everything is hot, frantic and stickily sweet. It's over the top
in every sense.

And the bottom line is – would you take out an important
insurance policy, or even subscribe to a magazine, as a
response to letters like these?

Frankly, we're puzzled

To quote an extremely well-known direct mail shot that
arrives when you haven't replied to the chance to win a
fortune: frankly, we're puzzled. We're puzzled about
whether this sort of in-your-face direct mail works at all these
days, let alone well enough to make it pay.

On the one hand, let's assume that companies wouldn't
waste their money on something that produces little or no
results. But on the other hand we've never met anyone who
says they have used the pen to fill in the form.

Everyone we speak to says that they call it junk mail, and
believe that the writers have thrown all real information,
respect and service straight in the bin. And so that's where
the reader puts the direct mail letter.

We wonder sometimes if it's because the technology exists to
research, produce and 'personalise' mass mailshots, that they

seem to be ever on the increase. In other words, is it because
it is possible rather than because they work?

Define success
Direct mail aficionados treat their letters like a science. All
the gimmicks mentioned above – the opening query or
scenario, the formula P.S. reminder, the capitals, bold letters
and exclamations, the additional message on the envelope,
the incentive bauble, the repetition – these are all supposed to
yield impressive business results. The claim is that it's
proven and established.

That's true, if you accept a conversion rate of 1–2% as
successful and proven. But apart from these 'conversions',
what impression are the other 99% left with? If they're
anything like us they feel completely alienated, harbouring a
mixture of contempt at the way they're spoken to, and
revulsion at the shocking waste of paper. Imagine throwing
99 out of every 100 sheets of paper in the bin and then calling
this a successful activity.

The industry has dug its heels in and churned out millions of
letters to the formula that a few organisations pioneered very
successfully in the USA many years ago. But we're now in
the third millennium. We have highly sophisticated
databases and other IT sifting and sorting devices at our
disposal. Yet the old campaigners still wield their clutch of
precious totems and continue to serve us up the same old
diet of corn and cheese.

What has changed?

Fortunately these dinosaurs are becoming old news. The

mind-set that makes them try and cajole, manipulate and shout at customers in order to flog us their products and services, is following the other dinosaurs. Things have changed and traditional direct mail looks increasingly impoverished and superfluous.

What has happened to accelerate the modern move towards warmer, more service-orientated business writing? Why do organisations take more time to pitch their tone correctly for customers? And why does the 'hard sell' approach have less and less impact in the marketplace, across all customer segments?

There are three key reasons:

1 Customers have become more sophisticated and have more information
Go to any focus group where customers are talking about their experiences with companies, and you'll hear the same kind of objections:

- companies talk to me as though I was born yesterday

- they show no interest in service beyond selling the product
- they're overheated before the sell, but stone-cold later when I need help
- they call me 'valued' yet it's quite clear that my name has been lasered in (and spelt wrongly)
- they don't value my relationship with them . . . and so on.

2 They know what they want and they know what you're up to
Today's customers understand the old marketing tricks all too well. Many customers can explain to you exactly why a certain product has been marketed in certain ways, and why it is or isn't effective. They're happy to give you a critical appraisal because they're wise to the hype and the gimmicks. What they want is real service, and with new entrants into the traditional marketplace and vastly increased choice they can afford to be more exacting than ever before.

3 Technology is leaving the 'push' approach to selling behind
When consumers didn't have much choice, companies could ignore customers' views. Customers gladly bought whatever they pushed out – a 'push' economy.

But in recent years – particularly with the advent of the Internet and e-commerce – service providers have mushroomed, distribution channels have exploded, communication and information has proliferated. There are now so many offerings of every service and product that the difficulty isn't so much getting hold of the product, as deciding which particular shape, colour, flavour, smell, features, length and finish to buy. You now go to the provider and say 'I'll take this, but not these'.

It's the same with information: instead of making do with what's available locally or even nationally, you can now pull

down what you want from a global source. In fact, the Internet is the archetypal 'pull' system – a vast pool of information that constantly grows and changes, from which you draw what you want.

So the style of our spoof DM letters relies on you not having much of a choice. It shouts at you instead of whispering; it attacks the senses instead of pleasing them; it instructs rather than informs. These days most people want a bit of respect, some clear information and good service and we are thinking longer and harder before giving our money for a product hawked in such dubious tones. And no matter how hard the technology tries to make a mass mailshot personal, it fails. A lasered signature is always just that, and the repeated use of a name or address in the text just gets annoying.

All this means that many people feel the writing is already on the wall for direct mail, mainly because e-commerce doesn't involve unsolicited rubbish falling through your front door. Electronic commercial services are more accessible, more controllable. And – crucially – you go to them when you want them, rather than having them thrust at you.

Can direct mail live on?

If direct mail is to continue to have any place at all in the modern business world, it must stop shouting and start listening.

The problem – language and tone
One of the themes in this book is, put yourself in a customer's shoes. It shouldn't be difficult but it does seem to be for many direct mail writers. Their view of empathy is that it makes you talk in headlines like: *It feels great having money in the bank, doesn't it . . . ?*

It may well feel great, but that's not necessarily a sentiment you want asserted to you in an unsolicited letter by a major bank.

Or an impressively-titled organisation asks you whether you have *Ever wondered how people make a fortune on the stock market?* You'll have seen plenty of examples yourself, of these cheesy, clichéd or formulaic devices.

Toning your direct mail: what to do
So how should we approach direct mail, if the aim is to re-establish it as an acceptable practice in the modern marketplace? The first thing to recognise is that you do not know any of the people you are writing to.

The second point is that different audiences are comfortable with a slightly different 'voice' in letters. So try and aim for a group with common factors, using marketing databases to select recipients with similar attributes, backgrounds and circumstances. It makes it easier to find common themes, and select language that the majority will find natural and easy to read.

Then think about these ideas. You will not be surprised to see that they have a lot in common with the best practice principles of business letters generally.

- Be respectful. Don't make assumptions about their thought or feelings. You are not their friend but they may allow you into their home for a moment. You are taking up their time in a busy world so be courteous.
- Be measured, not frantic – you're in a conversation, not on a soap box.
- Be level and consistent – not a mish-mash of styles (hot, then cold etc)
- Give information, not hype – people need *content* and help, to understand
- Instead of clichés and universal formulae, make it more personal
- Play down the product and play up service and customer benefits – and always talk benefits as well as just features

- Be open and honest, and avoid putting restrictions and exclusions in tiny print as a footnote at the end of the letter.

In other words, make your direct mail letters as similar as you can to any other business letter. It comes back down to the same guidelines we have looked at for all forms of writing.

Summary

Direct mail seems to be in a world of its own. It does not conform to the usual standards of business letters, and is in danger of becoming outdated for entirely different reasons.

Today we have looked at how to rescue direct mail, by bringing it back closer towards normal and everyday communication, reducing its outrageousness and making it more friendly and informative, less aggressive and instructing.

I am writing . . .

Today you are writing, because there is a good deal of scope to try out the techniques and principles covered throughout the week. This topic – business letters – is one that you can work on alone and with just a few examples to tackle.

So that's what today is all about. We will set out some examples and you have the chance to try out your own approach. We will show you what we would have done, but that doesn't mean there is only one answer. Your versions could easily be just as good as ours. Ultimately, as long as you are starting to move away from the formal and dusty style of traditional business letters and towards a more open, friendly and conversational style, that's fine.

Strong and active verbs

Earlier in the week we looked at a few examples of active and strong verbs, and we gave you four phrases to finish off in your own way.

Passive and active

Improving the originals is quite simple, and on the passive verbs we suggest:

Your card will be sent to you	*We will send you your card*
I have been informed that it has been arranged that your order will be delivered on Friday	*I now know that we have arranged to deliver your order on Friday*

Now, how about these? How could you rewrite these and make them active? Our suggestions are on the next page.

- *We have been informed by your bank*
- *Your payment will be collected by us each month*
- *Our price increases are set no higher than necessary*

Strong words

This is fairly straightforward as well. Our suggestions for the examples you looked at on Tuesday are:

We reached the conclusion that	means	*We concluded*
I have given consideration to	means	*I have considered*

Now, how about these? How could you rewrite these and make them stronger? Our suggestions are after the passive and active examples, on the next page.

- *The decision he made was to let it go*
- *The manager undertook a review in respect of her performance*
- *It's important to make a contribution.*

Our suggestions

For the active and passive we suggest:

We have been informed by your bank	*Your bank has told us*
Your payment will be collected by us each month direct from your account	*We will collect your payment direct from your account each month*
Price increases are set no higher than necessary	*We set our prices no higher than necessary*

For the stronger verbs we suggest:

The decision he made was to let it go	*He decided to let it go*
The manager undertook a review in respect of her performance	*The manager reviewed her performance*
It's important to make a contribution	*It's important to contribute*

Normal words for normal people

On Wednesday we looked at the benefits of using simpler – not more simplistic – words. We asked you to find replacements for these words, and suggested some possibilities.

- therefore   *so*

- concerning   *about*

- henceforth   *in future*

- endeavour   *try*

- signify   *mean*

- subsequent to   *after*

- for the duration of   *throughout*
- purchase [verb]   *buy*
- utilise   *use*

Try these now. The trick is to keep it simple – don't try and make it complicated just go with what comes into your head. We've left in the ones you have already done to give you a flying start.

- therefore
- endeavour
- for the duration of
- cessation
- signify
- henceforth
- by means of
- subsequent to
- sufficient
- ascertain
- commence
- due to the fact that
- purchase [verb]
- if this is the case
- with reference to

- in order to
- location
- assist
- concerning
- as a consequence
- forward [verb]
- obtain
- notify
- utilise

Remember, it all depends on the context, but some common replacements are:

• therefore	*so*
• endeavour	*try*
• for the duration of	*throughout*
• cessation	*end*
• signify	*mean*
• henceforth	*in future*
• by means of	*by*
• subsequent to	*before*
• sufficient	*enough*
• ascertain	*find out*
• commence	*start*

- due to the fact that   *because*

- purchase [verb]   *buy*

- if this is the case   *if so*

- with reference to   *about*

- in order to   *to*

- location   *site, place*

- assist   *help*

- concerning   *about*

- as a consequence   *as a result*

- forward [verb]   *send*

- obtain   *get*

- notify   *inform, tell*

- utilise   *use*

Going the whole way

Now let's try a couple of complete letters . . . both based on
real letters. We'll do a 'before and after' of each of them,
starting by setting out just the 'before'. Then you can work at
it on a piece of paper, before looking at our suggestions.

Letter 1 The original
A suggestion: read the letter and make sense of it in your
head first. Then imagine you are explaining what it says to
someone, face to face. When you write that down it will
almost certainly be a big improvement on the original.

Dear Mr Walker

I write with reference to my telephone conversation with Mr Smith on 15 July 1999, when he asked for details of your membership and informed me he had your permission so to do.

Pleased be advised that Mr Smith requested information to be sent direct to him but, due to the Data Protection Act, all past and current member information, whether financial or otherwise, is confidential. It must not be disclosed to any third party without the prior written consent of the member first being sent to the Club Secretary. In this case there was no prior written consent and, therefore, the information could be given.

At this club we take the confidentiality of member information extremely seriously. All our members expect us to treat their personal data confidentially. With this in mind, your details are set out on the attached sheet for your reference, the information that Mr Smith requested. If you wish to pass this information to Mr Smith that is entirely up to you. I trust, however, that you appreciate our position and agree that we cannot breach the confidentiality of our members in any way.

Yours sincerely

Letter 1 Our suggestion

Dear Mr Walker

I'm afraid I was not able to help Mr Smith when he phoned on 15 July asking us to send him details about your membership. This is simply to explain why, and to give the information to you personally instead.

We take the confidentiality of patient and member information very seriously indeed. Indeed, the Data Protection Act forbids us from disclosing any kind of personal information about a member to a third party, unless we first have that member's written consent. This applies whether you are a past or a present member, and whether the information is about financial or any other aspects of your membership.

So, because we did not have your written consent to disclose confidential data to Mr Smith, I had no choice. I had to explain that I could not send him the information he asked for.

However, there is nothing to stop me sending the information directly to you and you can pass it to him if you wish. I have put the details on the attached sheet for you.

I am sorry if this seems a little long-winded, but I feel sure you'll agree that it is important that we do not let our members down and risk giving out confidential information.

Yours sincerely

Now, you may find this a little strange at first, because it is quite a long way from the very formal tone of most business letters. It's certainly a million miles from the original but it does not get so friendly that it crosses the line and stops being businesslike. This is a club, after all, and we have taken that into consideration.

The facts are all there – The Data Protection Act, club policy and exactly what happened – but the tone is much more open, relaxed and conversational. There is more use of *I* and *you*, and much more active voice, because of the higher number of strong and active verbs. And we have used straightforward phrases and words, instead of the archaic ones in the original.

So while each individual change we made would not look significant on its own, when taken together the overall result is a drastically different letter. It really is much more like one modern adult talking to another.

Letter 2 The original
Now you get the chance to respond to a complaint about a holiday.

Dear Mrs Dooberry

I am writing in response to your correspondence concerning your holiday to The Algarve. Please accept our sincere apologies for the delay in our response. We would like to take this opportunity to offer our comments in a genuine endeavour to resolve this matter.

Firstly, we were extremely concerned to learn of the

dissatisfaction which you have expressed in relation to your accommodation at the Hotel Spliffo, as this is definitely not the type of reaction we wish to evoke from our clients.

I would point out that our brochure makes no reference to room service availability, and therefore we are surprised that you were led to believe this. All our members of staff use this as the basis for their own information so it seems unlikely that the information came from this source. However, if it did then we sincerely apologise. With this in mind, we have requested that all staff are reminded of the actual limitations of the various grades of hotel accommodation.

Whilst we regret that you had cause to write to us with your comments we would like to thank you for taking the time to do so. Your letter's content should help us to maintain future standards, and a copy of your letter has therefore been passed to our Contracting Manager in order that the details can be considered for the future.

I trust that this has answered your comments in full, but should you have any further questions or comments please do not hesitate to contact us.

Yours sincerely

H O'Liday

Letter 2 The revision

Now you get the chance to respond to a complaint about a holiday.

Dear Mrs Dooberry

I was very concerned to read that you did not enjoy everything about your recent holiday in The Algarve. I am sorry that it has taken some time to reply, but I wanted to investigate thoroughly for you.

We were grateful that you took the time to write, as we are always keen to hear of our customers' experiences. It helps us maintain and improve our service.

I am truly sorry if our brochure or any of our staff gave you the impression that room service was available at the Hotel Spliffo. I have checked the wording and can confirm that it does not mention room service, but I have passed your letter to our local representative in the resort and to our printing manager, so that we can be absolutely sure that it is clear in future.

All our staff rely on the descriptions in our brochure so it is extremely unusual for them to give out wrong information. We have reminded all our teams that they must stick to the brochure details, to reinforce the point strongly.

Once again, I am sorry that the lack of room service was a problem, but I hope that this did not spoil the rest of the holiday. Thank you again for writing, and if there are any other questions or comments I can help

---

> you with, please do call me at the number on top of this letter.
>
> Yours sincerely
>
> H O'Liday

The fundamental difference between the two is that the original talks down to the client like a teacher addressing a school pupil and gets defensive (almost *you must be wrong*) and then tries to turn on a sickly smile . . . *please do not hesitate to contact me* (which has gone in the revision, along with *I am writing to . . .*).

The original goes on far too long in places. It is certainly too apologetic when it drones on about *our sincere apologies for the delay . . . we would like to take this opportunity . . . a genuine endeavour to resolve this matter . . . extremely concerned . . . definitely not the type of reaction we wish to evoke from our clients . . .* Saying sorry is one thing, but prostrating yourself with grief is just a bit too much, especially as it`s unclear whether there's anything to apologise for.

The revision is actually more respectful despite being less of a grovel. It says *we regret you had a bad time* and it apologises if the company gave the client a false impression, but it is much more equal. It explains the position clearly without all the waffle in the original.

The main changes are from long-winded and unwieldy words and phrases, to more simple and straightforward alternatives. That, plus more active verbs and a more direct conversational approach, make a huge difference. The explanation is clearer, and it says exactly how the client's comments will help prevent the problem in future.

How do customers feel

But one acid test is whether this less formal style could upset some customers. We have to say, yes it could, especially dinosaurs in Edwardian spa towns who dream of the Empire and slowly munch cucumber sandwiches with the crusts off. But the vast majority of people strongly prefer it; we know because we have field-tested it. And actually more modern people disliked the original there than the number of dinosaurs who disliked the new version. So however you cut it, it's a winner.

Our final suggestion to you is in this same area. If you are not sure whether your customers prefer the old dusty and turgid style of letter-writing, or a modern, light and airy approach that treats them as equals and talks to them comfortably, give them a few before and afters, and ask them. It will all become clear.

Looking back over the week

Throughout this week we have taken to pieces the old approach to business letters, and rebuilt it so that it suits today's business scene.

We have looked at the way rules should help us create excellent communication, but when they are out-dated they can simply get in the way and defeat their own purpose. And

some of the bigger rules and conventions that have been around for decades – like keeping it distant, passive and cool – certainly need revising and updating for modern business writing.

Replacing tired words and phrases with simple and straightforward versions brings a touch of fresh air into letters, as does a more direct form of address that talks to the reader instead of at them. Treating people as adults with a brain should not sound novel, but it is a new approach in most businesses.

And the key to it all is to keep it conversational: to write as you would speak to a customer, with respect and yet with warmth, with openness and yet with politeness, with a smile but still with real concern for their problems, and a genuine desire to make your letter a positive contribution to a lasting relationship.